Contents

Acknowledgements

We wish to thank all the puppies that participated in the photo shoots for this book, they worked hard and we believe had fun posing for us. Thank you to their two legged family members for their time bringing them to the shoots and thank you to Hannah Wright who recruited the puppies for us and who assisted by helping the puppies to demonstrate the points we wished to illustrate. Without all of these inputs we could not have made the book what it is.

Dedication

This book is dedicated to all those who have taught us about dog behaviour over the years: teachers, colleagues, students and friends. As importantly, it is also dedicated to the dogs that came into our homes as puppies and who, in their growing up, have helped shape the concepts in the pages that follow.

Foreword by Jean Donaldson

Amid an explosion of training advice in books, on TV and in every corner of the internet – advice that ranges from alarming to nonsense to benign-but-missing-the bull's-eye – Helen Zulch and Daniel Mills have gotten everything right. And they've gotten it right on the most vital of all topics in applied behavior: rearing a puppy.

Puppy owners' time and energy are finite but the stakes are high, so these resources must be allocated carefully. Of the many virtues of *Life Skills*, the choices the authors make about what to include and what to omit are the most genius.

So how should we prioritize the tasks we need to accomplish with puppies? Owners obsess about potty training, and TV personalities obsess about physical intimidation cloaked in leadership mumbo-jumbo. What we should be most concerned with is fear, and we should be concerned for three reasons: 1) manifestations of fear in dogs include growling, snarling, snapping and biting, which have public safety implications as well as often carrying death sentences for the dogs; 2) getting dogs comfortable with the well-known list of things that may make them uncomfortable has time sensitivity attached to it, ie it is most readily accomplished in young puppies. In fact, squandering this time sensitivity can result in virtually indelible fear when, inevitably, life throws bad experiences at dogs. Resilience must be built – it is the 'padding' for when s**t happens; and 3) there are welfare implications attached to being anxious, afraid or uncomfortable about things one will encounter on a regular basis. The widespread failure of owners to read signs of stress in dog body language is of great concern: imagine feeling genuinely afraid and nobody noticing or caring, including your own family!

Life Skills never takes its eye off the build-resilience ball and the opportunity afforded by the plasticity of young puppies. And it gets the science right on this and every other topic – capitalizing on firsts, the necessity of gradual, incremental exposure, the order of events in Pavlovian conditioning, the power of noticing and differentially reinforcing behavior we want more of, the fact that there is no free lunch in behavior (dogs do what works), using contexts as cues for default manners-type behaviors, interpreting whether play is unfolding well (a notoriously mangled subject), those early signs of stress, and on and on. *Life Skills* gets the science right without once sacrificing accessibility. However critical this information is, it's useless if not transmitted in a sticky manner to owners and trainers on the front lines.

The crafty writing in *Life Skills* delivers hefty bang for buck. Take this sentence: "Because chasing is so inherently rewarding for dogs, teaching your pup to play safe, controlled games that incorporate chase – for example, with toys such as balls, Frisbees, tug toys, tuggies on a rope etc – can provide valuable stimulation which can increase his welfare." In this sentence, Zulch and Mills normalize normal behavior (chasing), myth-bust (tug is safe and even useful), fight fire with fire on the motivation front (predatory activity substituting for predatory activity), and pitch enrichment, which is a prime line of defense against boredom-induced behavior problems.

There are dozens of other themes and concrete examples that got me excited as I read, such as the value of giving dogs choices of multiple beds, and stopping on walks to allow sniffing. Heart be still that dogs can be granted this simple pleasure without us succumbing to a throe of insecurity about our status. Amazingly, even now, one can still read treatises in which adults with mortgages, cars and

Life skills for puppies

credit cards, and who can order every facet of their pet's existence, hand-wring about whether they are perceived as the dominant life form. We humans have built cities and filled museums with literally tons of art and artifacts, split the atom and sent spacecraft with dozens of instruments to orbit Saturn: don't worry, we're 'dominant.'

Zulch's and Mills' recognition that we've nothing to prove vis-a-vis our place in any hierarchy allows them to make the following point in the final chapter: puppies have the right to say 'no.' A huge piece of the puzzle for building a confident, friendly, well-mannered dog is that we notice and take proper action when a puppy feels worried or afraid. And this means respect, not coercion. Aside from empathy for the plight of a frightened dog, this has the practical benefit of avoiding his forced escalation. If we fail to see or heed the polite "no, please stop, that frightens me" of dogs, they will have no choice – like all properly functioning living organisms – but to give it to us in more desperate terms. In the case of dogs it will be with their teeth. The way to minimize the chance of this ever happening with your own puppy is in these pages. Read on!

Introduction

Sharing your life with a dog should bring immense pleasure and enjoyment, but all too often it results in frustration and even heartache instead. To maximise the chance of a long and happy relationship between you and your dog it is important that your pup learns what is expected of him, but also that his needs are met. Addressing these two aspects will help him to fit comfortably into modern human society.

It is important to realise that your pup is learning every waking minute of his day, both within your – and his – home, and also when he is out and about with you. Making sure that he learns the right way to behave in daily interactions is key to him growing into a good canine citizen. You and he can be helped to learn some of the skills needed for life if you enroll him in an appropriate puppy training class, although successfully raising a pup is about more than socialisation and training sessions.

Learning the right way to behave also means that instead of focusing only on obedience and obeying your commands, your pup begins to understand which is the correct choice to make in any context, and be able to choose to do it. A dog that can make these choices becomes a pleasure to have around, and this book aims to help you achieve this.

The philosophy behind this book is not to protect your pup from the stresses of daily life, but rather to teach him to be resilient so that he can cope with whatever the world throws at him. Life happens; he needs to be able to deal with it. We can help him cope by giving him choices, providing him with a safe haven within the home, and remembering that, when he is out and about with you, you are that safe haven for him. This book will help you to understand how to provide for all his behavioural needs, going beyond the provision of physical requirements, such as food and water, to ensure his wellbeing.

The book is divided into the ten key skills that we

Providing your puppy with a safe haven in your home is important, as it helps him cope with day-to-day stress by giving him a place to escape to if something worries him.

believe will enable your pup to cope with modern life. Each chapter covers a separate skill, giving a brief overview of the concept and why it is important, and then listing some tips for helping him to learn the skill. We have also included some suggestions for worksheets on which you can record your pup's progress (we suggest you photocopy these from the book). Please note that the skills should be developed simultaneously, and not consecutively.

In summary, this book will help you to help your puppy to learn the skills he needs for life, so that the risk of his developing problem behaviours is minimized, and the potential for a fulfilling relationship with you is maximised. Please note, it is not this book's aim to help you resolve serious behavioural problems with your dog, and it does not offer detailed training programmes for any behaviours except walking on a lead. If you need it, please seek the help of a suitably qualified professional in these areas.

Applying the concept of these Life Skills to raising your puppy doesn't mean additional time for training, but rather a commitment to a way of interacting with your dog that ensures his wellbeing, your enjoyment of him, and a fulfilling relationship for you both.

Please note that, for ease of reading, the text refers to the puppy as a male throughout, however, female is implied at all times.

Should you wish to find additional information regarding some of the techniques and procedures referred to in the book – for example teaching tug games and creating a safe haven – please visit the website for the University of Lincoln Life Skills Classes, www.lifeskillsforpuppies.co.uk .

By teaching your puppy skills for life you will build a stronger relationship with her.

I have confidence

Puppies – who are still young and forming their view of the world they live in – need to learn that all the things they will come across, both in the home and whilst out and about, are, on the whole, safe and nothing to be afraid of. Not learning to feel safe in their world puts them at risk of being frightened of certain things for the rest of their lives, which may result in some dogs behaving aggressively because they feel uncomfortable.

To build confidence two things are important: puppies need to experience all of those things they may come across during their lives, and they need to experience them in a way that is not frightening. Think of your puppy's

Remember that even everyday things can be scary if your puppy has never seen them before. Introduce new objects at a distance that your pup finds comfortable (watch her body language to check that she is relaxed), and even distract her with something pleasant, such as a toy, the first couple of times she sees something new. When using a distraction, do make sure that she first notices the novel item before becoming focused on the toy: she can't learn about something if she hasn't noticed it.
You can tell that this puppy is comfortable by noting the relaxed tail and face, as well as the playful posture.

LIFE SKILLS FOR PUPPIES

Ensure your pup's first meetings with other dogs are calm and controlled so that he is not frightened, and can learn safe and appropriate ways to greet. In this example a young pup is allowed to calmly approach a confident older dog which is known to behave well with puppies. Note that, in this case, the adult dog is held on a loose lead so that the situation can be more easily managed. The body language of both dogs indicates that they are comfortable and willing to interact.

early life experiences as laying a stable foundation that will enable him to grow into a confident, outgoing, friendly dog.

To maximise the chance of this, ensure that first introductions to new things, people and other animals occur at a distance or in a low-key way.

Try to imagine life from your puppy's perspective: the large, unknown dog galloping toward him may be friendly, but your puppy doesn't know that, and therefore could be frightened. If this happens a few times, your pup may begin to fear the approach of all dogs.

However, if you ensure that the first few times he meets another dog that the meeting is calm and quiet, and that your pup has a chance to move away if he wants to, then he should become resilient and confident about meeting strange dogs. Then, later, if a large dog does rush up to him, he should be able to cope with this.

Another example. If you would like your puppy to be comfortable with children, standing on the outskirts of a playground where he can sit and watch, and play with you or receive treats whilst children play in the distance would be a good first exposure. This way he can experience the sound of high-pitched voices and fast movement without feeling alarmed or overwhelmed.

If, the first time that he meets children he experiences them rushing up to him in an excited manner, leaning over and touching him, it may be so scary that he becomes frightened of children, even if they never actually hurt him.

Finally, remember that as dogs are a sociable species, learning to feel safe when left alone is a specific skill they need to master. By building short absences into your puppy's life at times when he is tired, fed and occupied with a safe chew or toy (one you feel confident leaving him with), he will gradually learn that being alone is not scary and that you will always come back to him. Always leave puppies in a safe, secure environment where they cannot harm themselves or inadvertently damage things.

TIPS
✦ Although puppies learn from every experience, the very first experience of something new is the most powerful, so it is critically important to ensure that the first exposure is a good one!

If the first occasion is not good, be prepared for a bad reaction the next time a similar situation occurs, but

Begin to leave your puppy alone for increasing periods of time to help her learn that being alone is not scary. Ensuring she has something good to occupy her when she is alone will help her to cope.

Life skills for puppies

give him a chance to adjust and learn. Remember, this is about giving him a foundation he can build on for life so be prepared to structure your next meeting even more carefully to aid this process.

✦ Make a list of all those things that your dog may need to get used to in his life and plan to introduce him to all of these within the first four months that you have him. For example –

- Vacuum cleaner
- Broom
- Hair dryer
- Car
- Shopping trolleys
- Bicycles
- Children
- Men with beards
- People wearing spectacles
- People wearing hats
- Black rubbish bags

Don't subject him to all of these at once, of course, or he may become overwhelmed and, in turn, frightened: the very thing you are trying to prevent.

✦ Make sure that each new experience is positive. Always begin exposure to a new experience in a low-key way: for example, switch on the vacuum cleaner when it is at the opposite end of the room, whilst a helper distracts the pup by playing with him, or gives him a special treat to chew on. Switch it off after a few seconds and wait a while before repeating the experience.

✦ One exposure is not enough. Although first experiences are the most important, it is vital that your pup has multiple

Noisy appliances can be particularly frightening for some puppies. Keeping your pup occupied with something pleasant, such as a chew, whilst the appliance is switched on at a distance can be very helpful in showing him a pleasant association with such objects. This will also reduce the risk of your pup getting into trouble through trying to pounce on a moving appliance (such as a vacuum cleaner) in play.

positive exposures to new things and situations, as these will build the foundation that gives him confidence in his world.

✦ If your pup reacts badly in any situation and does not recover quickly, remove him from it and reconsider how to introduce him. Don't get upset with him and don't make a fuss of him either; simply take him away from the situation and distract him by engaging his interest in something else.

Remember!

Never force your pup to interact with something he does not want to. Let him approach in his own time and give him the choice to move away. Don't make a fuss of him or what he is doing, simply make approaching the object/person more appealing by moving closer to it yourself and acting interested in it in a relaxed way, maybe touching the object, playing with one of his toys near it, or offering some tasty treats. If he really does not want to come any closer, try again another day. If he begins to look more relaxed, fuss him gently as a reward.

LIFE SKILL 1 WORKSHEET

My puppy has experienced the following –

Experience	Puppy's reaction	What I still need to do
example: Vacuum cleaner	Little wary but okay as long as cleaner on other side of room	Ensure door is open so he can leave; give him a toy/chew as distraction

I like surprises

Puppies can be surprised by many things – sudden noises, things that suddenly appear, or even an unexpected touch. When a pup is startled by something unexpected, it's very easy for the heightened awareness and focus which results to cause the pup to become fearful or anxious. To avoid this, help him to see that the unexpected thing or event is not scary, or, even better, help him to see

If you notice that your puppy looks worried when he encounters something, such as a loud noise, make a mental note to work on helping him to feel positive about it. Anxious or fearful body language can include having the tail tucked between his legs, lifting a paw, staring at the thing that has frightened him, and moving his body weight backward or even backing away. The puppy in this image is showing some of these signs.

If your puppy wants to take time to look at something (even things we don't believe are frightening can worry some dogs), allow her to do so. Letting her decide for herself, in her own way and time, that something is safe, helps her feel in control, and is an excellent way of reducing the risk of her developing fears later in life.

that it is in fact good. If pups are not given the chance to learn that unexpected things are usually positive, over time, he may begin to react fearfully (which could manifest as aggression) any time he is startled.

The most important thing you can do to help your pup deal with a situation that startles him (and that is not harmful) is to give him time to assimilate what is happening. A lot of pups will sit down and look at something that is out of the ordinary; some may run and hide, or even bark if they are really startled. Where possible, simply wait for your pup to get over his surprise in his own time. Don't fuss him, pick him up or tell him off, but simply wait quietly for him to settle down.

Once he has settled, gently encourage him to

approach the object, person or animal (if it is appropriate) at his own pace. If he is truly frightened, take him away from the situation with the minimum of fuss (don't comfort him, try not to touch him or lift him up, just gently encourage him to move away so that he can calm down in his own time), and plan how to set up a reintroduction (see Life Skill 1).

At the same time as ensuring that you appropriately manage surprises in daily life, you can also help him to view surprises as positives in themselves, rather than something toward which he needs to react negatively.

TIPS
✦ Think of the things that are likely to startle him

15

Opposite: Dogs who are surprised by a person when they are resting or are focused on another activity can react aggressively. Occasionally interrupting your puppy at such times to give him something really good, such as a tasty treat or a toy, can help him learn that people who surprise him are good. Of course, don't do this too often as he does need time to completely relax.

throughout his life and teach him that these are predictors of good things. For example, a puppy living with young children is likely to be approached when he is asleep on some occasions. Of course, children should be taught to never disturb a sleeping dog, but a responsible adult can teach the pup that being woken is a positive experience. When he is asleep, on occasion go to him with a highly desirable chew, food toy or prized treat. Gently touch him to wake him and immediately present the item to him.

✦ On occasions when he is settled with a toy or chew, walk up to him suddenly and present him with something he really likes. Do this particularly when he is really engrossed in what he is doing so that he is slightly startled, but will then associate surprise with a positive outcome.

✦ Without scaring him, on occasion create a sudden noise a short distance away from him (clatter a pan lid, drop a book), and immediately after the noise, drop a toy or a handful of treats near to him.

> ### Remember!
> Should you notice when you are going about your daily activities that he is startled by something, use it as an opportunity to interact with him in a happy, upbeat, playful way. The aim is to have him predict that "surprises can mean that good things happen."

Making a sudden noise – just enough to startle but not frighten him – and immediately afterward dropping some treats for him to eat will help him associate noises with positive things. Stop this immediately, though, if your puppy becomes scared, and seek advice from a suitably qualified professional.

LIFE SKILL 2 WORKSHEET

Preparing my puppy for life's surprises –

Situation/incident	My reaction	Puppy's reaction	What I still need to do
example: Crashing noises at a construction site	Kept walking	Jumped & looked around	Act in a way that shows him I am not concerned

I like to be touched

Puppies need to learn to tolerate handling of all parts of their bodies by their owners as well as by strangers (vets and groomers, for example). With most puppies this is easily and readily learnt, as touch, in the main, will be a pleasurable experience for them. Continue to gently handle your dog all over his body throughout his life to help him remain tolerant of handling as a safe and pleasant experience.

To help your puppy learn to enjoy being handled, gently touch him and then feed him a treat. If you follow each touch with a treat, touching begins to have a positive association in your puppy's mind. Ears and feet are often areas that puppies least like to be touched, so be sure to work on those areas with particular care and patience.

LIFE SKILLS FOR PUPPIES

TIPS

✦ In the early days after your pup has arrived, handle your pup at times when he is most likely to tolerate it well. For example, when he is very relaxed after a good game, or a walk and a meal and is ready to settle down. Sit on the floor with him and gently stroke him all over, building in holding each foot, feeling between his toes, gently rubbing his ears, lifting his lips, raising his tail, etc.

✦ Another opportunity to teach puppies to enjoy handling is when they are playing. If they are busy tugging on a toy, handling them can become part of the game, and therefore

REMEMBER!

If at any point he objects to touch simply back off a little and go slowly in that area, touching him more gently and only for short periods. If he wriggles, try not to let him go but try to get him to stay with you and settled, perhaps using a different type of touch, or one that you know he likes. We don't want him to learn that if he wriggles you will let him go immediately, but neither do we want to panic him if he is finding being touched scary (see later).

Sometimes, when your pup is enjoying a game, stroke her on different parts of her body, which again helps to build a positive association with being handled.

This puppy is showing mixed feelings about being handled: note the arched back and stretched out front legs as he pulls away slightly whilst still focusing on the treat. If you see this type of response, make things easier for your pup for a while by reducing the intensity of handling. For example, go back to simply stroking his ears without trying to lift them.

build a positive association. You will still need to teach tolerance of touch when he is calm and relaxed, but it may be easier for some pups to accept it if they have already experienced this during play.

✦ Once he will tolerate gentle touch all over, on some occasions make your handling slightly firmer, say, the way a vet may do if he were examining your pup. You can also do things such as open his mouth and pop a treat inside, or gently squeeze his nails one at a time whilst feeding him treats, so that he becomes used to the actions that accompany giving pills and nail clipping.

✦ If there are areas of his body that he will not allow you to touch, seek help from a specialist who can advise you how to counter-condition him to such handling. NEVER force

him to accept touch (unless of course it is an emergency situation), and never punish him for not wanting to be touched. It is only with care and patience that he will come to understand that touch is a good thing.

Remember!
All dogs should be taught to accept brushing from young, and this is particularly important for long-coated breeds. It's better to spend a minute every day brushing a little of your pup's body than to try to do it all at once, as even pups who do not dislike being brushed may try to bite at the brush in play. Distracting him for a short period whilst you briefly brush him should enable you to build up to full brushing in quite a short space of time.

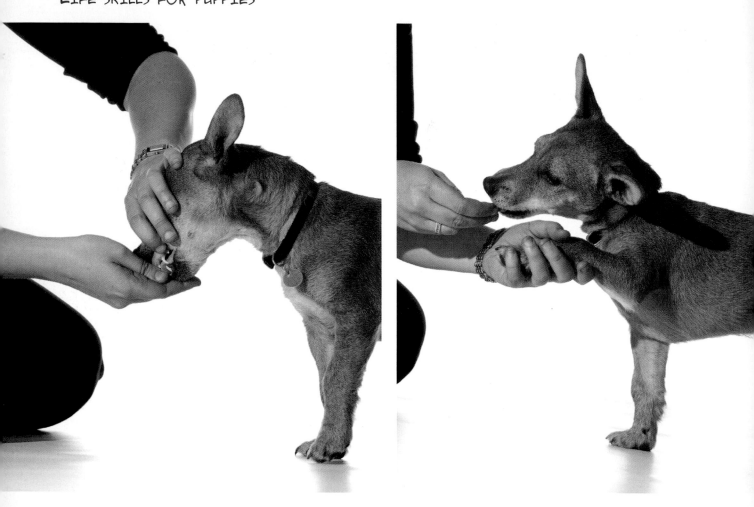

Once your puppy is very relaxed about being touched gently all over his body, begin to get him used to more invasive and firmer handling, the sort a vet might need to use.
In these pictures the puppy is learning to tolerate having his mouth opened and firm pressure on his paw.

LIFE SKILL 3 WORKSHEET

My puppy has been handled by me and others –

Parts of my pup's body handled
example: Front feet

Puppy's reaction
Pulled them away

What I still need to do
Practice holding his feet gently when he is lying down (feeding treats for not pulling away), and gradually progress to lifting his feet when he is standing

I can't do everything I want, when I want to; I don't expect to get everyting I want, when I want it

Being able to exercise self-control and tolerate frustration are two really important skills for puppies to master. Dogs who are impulsive, or who become easily frustrated often exhibit behaviours that are difficult to live with, or even dangerous: for example, impulsively grabbing at something someone is holding because they want it, or showing aggression as a result of being thwarted in their desire to get to something.

Self-control

The key feature of self-control is that the appropriate and desirable behaviour is under the control of the dog, who is

Going for a walk is exciting for most dogs, so sitting calmly to have their lead attached takes a great deal of self-control. In the beginning, teach your pup to sit for the lead to be clipped on and off at different times, and in a number of situations. In this way it becomes easier for her to show self-control at exciting times because the calm behaviour has already been established.

24

choosing to behave in a controlled manner as opposed to being controlled by a person telling him what to do all the time. Although obedience is also important (see Life Skill 7), self-control is vital.

Situations where dogs need to exercise self-control include –

- When greeting people – so they don't jump up
- When playing games – so that they don't grab toys and inadvertently cause injury
- When leaving the house or a vehicle – so they remain calm enough to have a lead attached if necessary, and go through a door in a safe manner
- Around food – so they are not jumping up at or onto counters or table tops, or trying to take food from people's plates
- Any time when they may be excited – so that they can behave appropriately and not injure themselves or a person, or cause damage (by chasing moving objects or jumping up, for example)

TIPS
✦ Initially you will need to teach your pup the appropriate behaviour for different situations; for example –

- Ask him to sit to be greeted
- Teach him to wait to be invited to go through doorways
- Teach him to wait to be invited to take a toy rather than try to grab it

✦ Once he understands what is expected of him, stop asking him to sit or wait or leave the toy, simply wait until he offers the behaviour before you greet him, open the door, give him the toy. If he does not offer the behaviour you expect, simply walk away from him and wait a little while before trying again. If he makes a mistake more than twice you should assume it is too difficult for him to do the correct thing at this point, so go back to making it easier by asking him or by working at a time when he is less excited/tired and more able to concentrate properly.

In the beginning you will need to teach your pup to sit, and then ask her to sit for something she would like, such as her toy. After a while, when you have something she wants, wait for her to offer to sit without asking. In this way she learns that the quickest way to get something that you have (and she wants) is to sit politely instead of jumping or grabbing; both of which are annoying and potentially dangerous behaviours.

✦ Be sure that when you notice your pup exhibiting self-control you do reward him. For example, if a visitor has just arrived and he has sat politely at their feet ready to say 'hello,'

tell him how good he is and either ask the visitor to gently greet him (so as not to over-excite him) or, if this is not appropriate for some reason, praise him and give him some fuss yourself.

The more he learns that controlling his desires leads to access to good things, the more likely he is to continue to do so.

25

LIFE SKILLS FOR PUPPIES

If your pup sits to greet people, ensure that he is acknowledged and receives attention for this, otherwise he may jump up to get attention.

✦ Some games can be used to help your pup learn self-control: tug, for example, is very useful. Firstly, get your pup interested in tugging on a suitable toy – most dogs seem to find the fleece tugs attractive. Once he is tugging well, teach him to release the toy by showing him a treat, giving it to him when he drops the tug to get it. When he is predicting that a second hand moving towards him will deliver a treat,

I can't do everything I want, when I want to; I don't expect to get everything I want, when I want it

Teach puppies to give up items they have in their mouths by first exchanging a toy in their possession for a treat or another desirable toy. Initially show your pup the treat, as in these images, but later, when she is quickly dropping the item as your hand moves toward her, advance an empty hand. In this way she learns to give something up without first seeing a reward. Remember to still reward her for letting go with something you have hidden out of sight. At this point you can also add the cue 'drop,' or similar.

Some puppies need to learn this swap initially when they are fairly calm and then later introduce the concept when they are in the midst of a good game. Letting go of something they are actively tugging on takes a great deal of self-control.

say 'give' (or equivalent) as you move your hand toward him and he should release the toy.

Once he has learnt to enjoy tugging and to release when asked, we can teach him the self-control of not trying to grab the toy unless he has been invited. Initially, just stand and hold the tug where he can see it, but not within reach. Any movement he then makes away from the toy – be it a step away, sitting down, or moving his head away – praise him and give a cue to take the toy, at the same time moving the toy toward him. Practise this, gradually making the toy more exciting and desirable, but still in the expectation that he will NOT grab the toy until he has been invited to do so. Any time he tries to grab it without invitation, simply move the toy out of reach and move away from your puppy. Remember, we are expecting him to learn self-control, and the correct response in the situation, which is not to take things unless he is invited to.

✦ Teaching your pup to walk nicely on the lead is also a very good way to encourage him to control himself. If you think of it from your pup's perspective, most things that are happening when he is out on a walk are exciting, making it hard for him to want to remain close to you, and yet he can learn to walk nicely next to you, controlling his desire to pull toward everything he wants to investigate. See the Appendix on teaching loose lead walking. Always remember, the function of the lead is to PROTECT, not to control. Your dog should be in control of himself, taking responsibility for being by your side, not being held there by force exerted through the lead. However, you must always ensure that your dog can sniff and investigate as you go, which is entirely natural canine behaviour from which all dogs derive pleasure and mental stimulation.

Frustration
Puppies need to develop frustration tolerance and an ability to cope with disappointment. If a dog becomes very frustrated he can display problematic or even dangerous behaviours, including aggression (especially when he is restrained or confined in some way), destructive behaviour, and noisy behaviour, such as excessive barking.

A number of situations can be manufactured to help your pup learn to cope with not being able to have

It is important to teach your pup not to grab at something in your hands simply because she wants it. This again demands a great deal of self-control. This pup has learnt that the only way to get the tug toy is to wait calmly until she is told she can have it.

Teaching your pup to walk politely on a lead without pulling helps him to exercise self-control. In these situations he would probably much rather engage in activities that he finds more rewarding, such as rushing ahead to sniff something interesting, or greet someone.

something he wants so that he does not become frustrated, and learns to remain calm and in control of himself in the face of disappointment.

TIPS
✦ Once you have taught your pup to walk nicely on the lead you can begin to teach him how to cope with the disappointment of not always getting where he wants to go when he is on the lead.

REMEMBER!
At all times build this skill slowly as pushing your pup beyond his ability to cope may in fact cause frustration and develop unwanted behaviours, rather than teaching the skill you desire.

✦ Start off with something easy for him. For example, ask a friend to place a favourite toy or treat on the ground, or ask someone that you know your pup would like to greet to simply stand in one spot. Take your pup just close enough

This pup is being taught that it is rewarding to pay attention to her owner rather than try to pull toward something on the ground that she wants. Teaching puppies in a positive way that they won't always get everything they want helps them to learn to cope with frustration.

LIFE SKILLS FOR PUPPIES

for him to notice the toy or person, but not so close that he gets too excited about it. Stop and wait for him to relax and, if possible, look at you, then turn away from what he wants, encouraging him to go with you. When he does, make a big fuss of him and offer him another toy or treat which he was unaware you had. Then turn back toward the toy or person and, giving him a release cue (such as 'go get it' or 'say hello' if you are releasing him to greet a person or dog, take him quickly to the reward. Move quickly enough that he doesn't pull you.

Practise this, getting closer and closer to the original toy or person before asking him to choose to leave the thing he can see and wants. Vary the object/person/other friendly dog and sometimes expect him to walk on by or turn

> ### REMEMBER!
> It is normal for a puppy to like chasing moving objects (cars, bikes, joggers, cats, etc). Always take something he really likes, either a toy or treat, on any outing where he may come into contact with something he may try to chase so that you can teach him to direct his attention to you rather than become frustrated by being prevented from chasing.

away and NOT get it. In this way he learns that not getting something he wants is not the end of the world.

Use the ideas in the points above to teach your pup to cope with the frustration of not being able to chase moving objects and animals. Choosing not to chase something he would like to involves self-control; showing restraint when faced with something he would like to chase involves frustration tolerance.

✦ Feed your pup some of his meals or his usual treats in a food toy, such as a Kong™. Start with easy to empty toys, gradually introducing those that he needs to put more effort into getting the food from. This won't teach him to give up something that he wants, but it will teach him to remain calm and focused in the face of a struggle for something he wants, and to cope with having a reward delayed.

This puppy is eating some of her meal from a safe food dispensing toy. Having to work to obtain food from toys helps pups to cope with a delay in accessing a desired reward, and also provides mental stimulation. To ensure that you do not CAUSE frustration, take care that your pup can cope with the level of difficulty of the toy you give her and, in addition, remember that you may need to show her how to use it.

✦ Teach him to understand that attention is not always available (see Life Skill 5), but that he can amuse himself even if he would rather interact with you. Again, this helps him to cope with disappointment.

✦ Occasionally, shut your pup behind a barrier so that he learns to cope with being contained in this way. The first few times you do this, make sure it's at a time of day when he has had a walk or a game, a meal and is ready to settle down.

Make sure that he has a comfy bed, some safe toys and fresh water, and leave him alone for a short while – either in his crate, puppy pen or behind a gate or door.

In the beginning, leave him only for a short period, and gradually extend the time he is alone. If he does whine or bark, wait until he settles down, and only then allow him to rejoin you but without making a fuss of him. This helps him learn how to deal with the frustration of having a barrier between himself and something he wants.

✦ Make sure that all of your pup's needs are met (see Life Skill 10), especially his need to channel excitement and arousal into suitable outlets – such as safely chasing and tugging at suitable toys.

✦ As you work to help your pup develop these skills, the objective should be for him to be able to relax in the face of disappointment, rather than simply tolerate it in a state of expectation. When he can do this, not only is his immediate behaviour more appropriate, but his welfare is also improved.

A few words about chasing

As already noted, almost all dogs will initially try to chase fast moving objects, given the chance. As this usually means wildlife, cats, livestock, joggers, cyclists and motorised vehicles, it's generally the case that such behaviour is unacceptable, and possibly even dangerous.

PLEASE REMEMBER

• NEVER take a chance – if your dog would put himself or a person or another animal at risk should he chase, keep him on the lead.

• Don't allow him to practise chase behaviour before you have completed his training. Chasing is fun, and once he learns this – and that he can ignore you when he is chasing – you will find it a lot harder to teach him not to chase and to control him should he start to do so. In the short term this may mean not walking your pup near roads if he wants to chase traffic; not allowing him off lead in woodland if he wants to chase squirrels, etc.

This pup has been taught that her crate is a safe, comfortable place where she can relax. Teaching puppies to tolerate being shut away from people, or something else that they want, is a very important skill as otherwise they may grow up unable to tolerate the frustration that a barrier causes.
Pups who know that their crate is a place where only good things happen (such as treats, chews and toys) also have an automatic safe haven to retire to if they are worried by things in their environment.

• Teach him to come back when you call him, immediately, every time, as well as alternative behaviours to chasing (see internet sites and training books for information on teaching reliable or emergency recall cues, as well as teaching alternative behaviours).

Cyclists, joggers and other fast-moving targets will trigger a chase response in most dogs. Until she has learnt self-control, at any time when your puppy is in a situation where she may want to chase, keep her on a lead so that she cannot practise this undesirable and potentially dangerous behaviour.

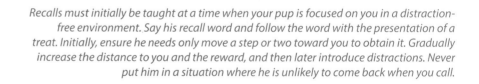

Recalls must initially be taught at a time when your pup is focused on you in a distraction-free environment. Say his recall word and follow the word with the presentation of a treat. Initially, ensure he needs only move a step or two toward you to obtain it. Gradually increase the distance to you and the reward, and then later introduce distractions. Never put him in a situation where he is unlikely to come back when you call.

- If you already have a confirmed chaser you may need additional help from a behaviour or training specialist.

- Because chasing is so inherently rewarding for dogs, teaching your pup to play safe, controlled games that incorporate chase – for example, with toys such as balls, frisbees, tug toys, tuggies on a rope – will provide valuable stimulation which can increase his wellbeing.

Most dogs enjoy tug games and chase games (for balls, frisbees or other appropriate toys). These games are beneficial as long as they are played according to consistent rules. Spend some time every day playing safe games with your puppy as this will help to channel her natural desires in appropriate ways.

LIFE SKILL 4A WORKSHEET

LEARNING SELF-CONTROL

My puppy has practised self-control –

Situation	*Puppy's reaction*	*What I still need to do*
example: Sitting for his meals	Will sit without being asked, as long as no other dogs around	Feed in a different room if other dogs around so he can show self-control

I can't do everything I want, when I want to; I don't expect to get everything I want, when I want it

LIFE SKILL 4B WORKSHEET

LEARNING FRUSTRATION TOLERANCE

My puppy has practised frustration tolerance –

Situation	Puppy's reaction	What I still need to do
example: Bathroom door shut whilst I shower	Barks and scratches at door	Give him a chew or toy to keep him occupied outside the bathroom before I take a shower. Obtain a see-through barrier (child gate?) as an intermediate measure

I can be calm

As well as providing enough stimulation for your puppy in the form of games, toys, gentle walks and training sessions, it is important for your pup to learn to relax, amuse himself, and calm down if over-excited.

Whilst there is nothing intrinsically wrong with giving your puppy attention when he asks for it, it is important that he is not inadvertently taught to want constant attention from people, as this needy behaviour can cause tension in your relationship. However, being able to settle down quietly or to go off and amuse himself appropriately are skills which need to be taught. Additionally, being able to calm down when he is already excited is a very important skill for him to learn, as overexcited dogs can put themselves and others at risk.

Teaching your pup to calm down when excited, and to amuse himself calmly during some periods of the day, means you won't have to constantly curb him and tell him off for annoying or dangerously over-excited behaviour. Better for him, better for you, and better for the precious relationship you have.

TIPS

✦ Ensure that your pup has some quiet time each day, after he has had some form of exercise or stimulation (a walk, a game, some training), and has eaten and been to the toilet. Take him to his bed or put him in his puppy pen or a quiet room, and provide him with a special food toy or chew, also ensuring that some of his other favourite toys are available to him.

Use a word (such as 'settle') when you walk away from him, and make sure that for a period of time you do not interact with him – even if he asks for attention (keep yourself busy with another task to resist the temptation

There are numerous food toys on the market. Invest in a selection of these, choosing those which your pup is unlikely to be able to chew into pieces and swallow. Teach him to use the toys and present them to him in rotation. In this way he can be kept occupied, and learn to amuse himself independently of you.

Settling quietly and calmly on his bed or in his special space is an important skill for a puppy to learn. Help him to find this behaviour rewarding by initially providing him with a suitable food toy when you ask him to settle.

to give in to him). After a while (brief initially, but slowly increasing) go to him and invite him to you for some calm attention; gentle stroking, quiet interaction, etc. Over time he will begin to understand that when you use 'that word' he must quietly amuse himself, or settle down for a rest.

✦ Teach him to calm down when he is excited by making it part of a game. When playing with him, sometimes take a food toy or a handful of treats and interrupt the game with a word, such as 'enough,' then quickly get his attention and give him the toy or scatter some treats on the ground at your feet. When he has finished with the distraction item

REMEMBER!
Once you have asked him to settle down, make sure that it's YOU who initiates the next interaction. If you allow him to badger you into giving him attention, he will soon learn that your cue to go and amuse himself has no meaning.

and is much calmer, sometimes begin the game again, with another word or phrase, such as 'let's play.' Other times, just walk away from him to show that the game is over. In

LIFE SKILLS FOR PUPPIES

this way you will teach him an 'off switch' for when he gets excited.

✦ After a number of repetitions you can begin to phase out the distraction item and just give him quiet attention until he calms down. In this way he will learn that when you use the word cue he must quieten down – and no-one ever needs to get upset with him!

This puppy is enjoying an exciting game of tug. Her owner then cues 'enough' (top right) and drops a few treats, so the puppy stops playing to eat. In this picture she is still quite aroused after the game, but in the third picture (bottom right) is becoming calmer and more relaxed. Once she is totally relaxed the game can be re-started, should her owner wish.

Remember!
One of the key points here is to ensure that on those occasions when you want to resume the game, she is completely calm before you do so. If you resume the game before she is calm, she won't learn the skill of actually becoming less excited.

LIFE SKILL 5 WORKSHEET

I CAN BE CALM

My puppy has practised amusing himself –

'Settle' practice	*Puppy's reaction*	*What I still need to do*
example: Tried when he was a little tired	Seeks attention as soon as food toy is empty	Try again when he is very tired

....

....

....

....

....

....

....

My puppy has practised calming down when excited –

'Enough' practice	*Puppy's reaction*	*What I still need to do*
example: Will stop playing & redirect attention to treats	Seeks attention as soon as food toy is empty	Remain firm in not engaging again until he has settled

....

....

....

....

....

....

....

I know (and can follow) the rules

Canine and human societies differ in a number of areas, and some of the traits which, through many years of breeding, we have selected dogs to have may actually turn out to be problematic. For example, dogs naturally greet muzzle to muzzle, and because one trait we have selected is friendliness to people, this may be why a natural response of most dogs to greeting a person is to jump up to get close to their face. Dogs also tend to naturally seek comfort, and are opportunistic in that they will take advantage and help themselves to things they may want, and which appear to be available to them. This, coupled with a lack of understanding about the consequences of, for example, muddy paws on furnishings or helping themselves to the roast on the kitchen counter, may well lead to conflict with their families.

The best way to avoid conflicts like this is to teach your pup what is expected of him from the moment he enters the house and becomes part of the family. It's very easy to make allowances for a cute, eight-week-old bundle of fluff, without appreciating that what is learnt initially usually makes the strongest impression and is thus hardest to change.

TIPS
✦ Decide on a set of house rules that ALL family members and visitors can adhere to at all times. Ideally, these should be decided before the pup even enters the house, and

These puppies are greeting muzzle-to-muzzle and then initiating a game. Muzzle greetings are normal in dogs, and in dog society it is polite for puppies to greet their elders in this manner. This may be why puppies frequently jump up at people in an attempt to get close to their faces.

41

Life skills for puppies

include all aspects of life, from which rooms the pup will have access to, to whether or not he is allowed on the furniture, and how he should behave around people or in the car.

✦ Put a copy of the list of rules on display somewhere readily visible in the house (for example, on the fridge door) so that all members of the family can be reminded to apply them consistently to help your pup learn.

✦ Taking just one of these areas as an example: there's no reason why the majority of dogs need be excluded from access to the furniture: with the rare exception, this does not lead to behaviour problems. However, if you decide to allow your dog uncontrolled access to the sofa and the beds, remember that –

- He won't know that his muddy paws will make the furniture dirty
- He won't understand that jumping up beside a baby or elderly relative may not be appropriate
- He won't understand that it's okay in your house but not in your friend's house when you go visiting

  For this reason it is usually a good idea to restrict access to an 'invitation only' basis, or to a special chair, or only when the chair is covered with 'his' blanket. To achieve this make sure that –

- As a pup, people give him attention on the floor, not lift him up onto the sofa next to them
- There is a comfy dog bed in the living area so that he can join the family in comfort on his own bed
- If you want to be able to invite him up with you on the sofa, do so at specific times, or when there is a specific cover on the chair, and use a specific word
- At all other times control his access to the furniture (close the door into the room, place a pile of books or

If you don't want your pup on the furniture when she grows up, rather than lifting her onto the sofa when she is tiny, teach her that the attention she wants will come down to her level. Do this by getting down on the floor with her to give her love and cuddles.

It is a good idea to post your list of house rules in a prominent place as this helps everyone in the family to be consistent in their interactions with your puppy.

HOUSE RULES

Furniture

- Dogs may get on conservatory furniture at any time – even if they are wet or dirty
- Dogs may NEVER be allowed on living room furniture
- Dogs may get onto beds only when invited

Gates, doors, etc
- Dogs must wait at every door or gate to be invited to go through

Visitors
- Dogs must sit to greet visitors

Providing a comfortable dog bed in the areas where you spend time will allow your pup to keep you company, and at the same time make it easier for her not to try to climb onto your invitingly soft sofa.

magazines on the seat), and if you find him there without being invited, gently ask him to get down whilst giving him minimal attention

• Make a quiet fuss of him when he is in his own bed at times when he has not been invited up with you

✦ Decide on a set of cues and instructions that everyone can understand and use. As dogs don't understand English, every cue must be distinct and have its own meaning. For example, if you plan to teach your dog to lie down on the

REMEMBER!
Whilst most rules can be decided by you and your family, society's opinion is important. For example, even a friendly dog can scare someone by jumping up at them, so the principle of 'sit to be greeted' is a sensible one.

cue word 'down,' you need to use a different word to mean 'get off the sofa,' otherwise if your dog is sitting on the sofa and you say 'down,' and he lies down instead of getting off, you shouldn't be angry with him as in his mind he has complied with your request. Rather use a word like 'off' or 'floor' to mean 'please get off the furniture.'

✦ Once you have set boundaries you must be prepared to enforce them. Don't ask for something in the early days of your relationship if you are not prepared to follow through and insist on it. This, of course, does not imply resorting to punishment or reprimand, or becoming angry, but simply ensuring that situations can be managed appropriately. It also implies that the pup understands the request and is able to do as asked.

✦ For example, imagine you want to teach your pup to wait until he is invited to get out of the car, rather than try to leap out at the first opportunity. This is an extremely important skill as, in an emergency – say a motorway hard shoulder – you need to know that he will not endanger himself or others by jumping out uninvited.

1

- Firstly, teach him to wait in the car (using food rewards) in a non-distracting environment, while you open and close the door
- Then teach him to get out when you ask
- Then practise this in different environments, and if he attempts to get out before he is invited to do so, simply close the door again until he is waiting calmly
- For the rest of his life ALWAYS invite him to get out of the car using his cue word. Any time he attempts or manages to get out without being invited, calmly put him back in the car, close the door, and keep him there until he is waiting politely and can be invited to get out

Learning not to rush uninvited through open doors or gates may one day save your puppy's life. In the following sequence of five photos, this puppy has been rewarded for sitting calmly in her crate, even when the door is opened. You can see how she is looking to her owner to be invited to come out.
You can drop food treats into the crate to reward your pup for good behaviour, whether the door is open or closed.

2

3

4

5

✦ Because we need to be able to enforce our requests, it is always important to –

- Think about whether or not what we are asking is sensible under the circumstances – for example, trying to call a young pup away from playing with his friends may be beyond him, so it may be more appropriate to manage the situation by going to fetch him rather than risk him learning to ignore your calls
- Manage situations where he may not be able to comply – keep him on the lead when he meets someone he is likely to jump up at so that you can help him not to make a mistake
- Practise for extreme situations – have friends play with their dogs next to your car (in a safe location) with the door open, whilst you feed him treats for not jumping out. Then when he is quiet and calm, invite him to get out to join them

✦ It is much easier for your dog to learn what you do want

him to do, rather than what you don't want. It is also quicker, in the long run, to teach him in this way. For example, teaching your dog 'don't greet people inappropriately' is quite a difficult concept for him, and may mean many months of us stopping first one type of unwanted greeting behaviour, and then another.

Even if he learns that putting his paws on people receives a negative response, he may still leap around them, bark at them or grab at their clothes because it's exciting and rewarding in its own right. However, if he is taught to sit politely in front of a person he wishes to greet, by definition he cannot be doing anything which may cause a problem for the person or for him.

Think of everything you want your pup to learn and phrase it in the positive. For example –

- Sit for greeting
- Walk next to me
- Sit when I open the front door

REMEMBER!

Dogs do not understand the concept of 'no' because it can mean so many different things: for example, it may mean 'don't move' in one context and 'don't sit still' in another. In some cases, where it has often predicted punishment, dogs can come to actually fear the word. For this reason teaching your pup the concepts of 'leave it alone' and 'give it to me' are much better ways of controlling behaviour than simply saying 'no.'

Initially, ask your puppy to sit every time he approaches a person he may want to greet, and then have that person reward him with a treat and their attention. Later, he will begin to sit without being asked, at which point make sure he gets attention when he does so that the behaviour is strengthened. If he is ignored when he sits in front of someone, he may well revert to jumping up to gain attention.

Eventually, you can call him, or use your 'enough' or 'leave it' cues to move him calmly away from people who really don't want to greet him.

✦ If you don't want him to do something, don't let him practice it (but don't deny him the opportunity to learn self-control over it; see Life Skill 4). This may mean managing situations until he has the self-control to manage himself.

For example, if you want him to learn to play appropriately with children without nipping and clawing, introduce him to first playing alongside them with his own toys when the children are calm. If they're running about wildly, place him in a separate room or his pen or crate with a really desirable chew or food toy to keep him occupied.

✦ Encourage behaviours you *do* want by rewarding him with praise, attention, petting, food or a game. Puppies learn from every experience, so make sure they learn what you want them to. For example, when playing games is a really good time to teach your pup useful skills such as 'give it to me' and 'only take it when I tell you you can.'

✦ The only way a puppy is going to learn the rules is if they are applied with absolute consistency, which is why they need to be decided and agreed on by ALL family members.

Previously, we have illustrated how to teach your pup to drop a toy in exchange for a treat. It is also important to teach your pup to drop other treasured items when requested, and the following three photos illustrate how your pup can be taught to give up a desirable chew in exchange for another chew or a special toy.

47

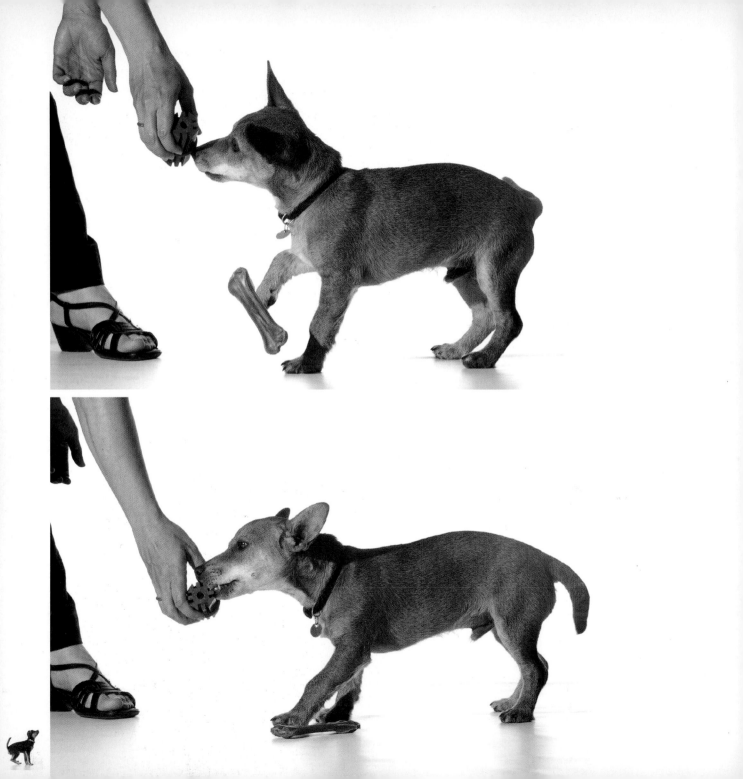

Note the wary expression on this puppy's face as a hand comes toward her chew. In the second image she is more relaxed, but in image three (overleaf) she again looks a little concerned. This type of body language tells you that you need to practise lots of exchanges of one desirable item for another that is even more desirable. In this way your pup will learn that a hand approaching when she has something important to her does not mean loss. Practising this and then moving on to teaching the 'drop' cue will help prevent your puppy developing defensive behaviour around things she believes are hers.

Remember!
The same behaviour by your dog must elicit the same response from people every time!

Thinking that it's okay if he does something he shouldn't 'just this once' simply confuses him, and means that the rule will be learnt more slowly or not at all. This is particularly true if the thing he is allowed to get away with is intrinsically reinforcing – such as attention from the person he has jumped up against or the comfort of lying on the nice soft sofa in front of the fire!

✦ Positive training does not mean being permissive; discipline must be maintained in a kind manner.

The idea behind teaching your pup boundaries should not involve constantly nagging him to do or stop doing things, but to make the rules so clear that, most of the time, he adheres to them without needing to be asked, and when you do need to ask something specific that he obeys readily and happily. Puppies need boundaries to be established and rules to be consistently and fairly applied to help them learn where there is comfort, and so that they become confident and relaxed, and grow into dogs who are a pleasure to have around.

However, it is important to remember that when dogs do something we don't approve of, it is not done through spite or a desire to 'get back' at us, but simply because it works for the dog at that time. It gets him something he wants or which makes him feel better.

Of course, if your pup has already learnt some habits that you would like him to lose, it's not impossible to achieve this, although it may take longer and require more patience on your part. It will also require more careful management of situations in the short-term to help him to get it right, rather than make mistakes. For example, ensuring you close doors into rooms, or keep him on a lead to meet people.

If you are struggling to change your pup's behaviour, or are in doubt as to how to manage situations, it is advisable to seek help from a reputable animal behaviour specialist.

LIFE SKILL 6 WORKSHEET

Rules in our house and for our lifestyle –

example: Puppy is allowed in all of the rooms except the baby's bedroom

. . . .

. . . .

. . . .

. . . .

. . . .

. . . .

. . . .

. . . .

Cue words and what they mean: our dog's dictionary –

Word	**Meaning**
example: 'Sit'	*Put your bottom on the ground immediately*

. . . .

. . . .

. . . .

. . . .

. . . .

. . . .

. . . .

I can listen

The previous Life Skill, where we teach a dog to understand the rules, is centred around your pup managing his own actions, or, in other words, being well behaved. This skill, of being able to listen and respond to requests, overlaps but is different in that it focuses on the pup's compliance to requests that may sometimes differ from the already established rules and boundaries.

For example, an existing rule may stipulate that, on a walk, the puppy may wander anywhere he likes as long as he remains in view, but instant compliance may be required if a deer suddenly jumps out in front of him, and you need to ensure that he does not give chase.

Although obedience training per se may not prevent problem behaviours, a dog that responds quickly and correctly to cues (requests) is easier to control in all situations, and therefore easier to integrate into daily life. An obedient dog that completely understands the consequences of responding to requests is also more likely to be confident about interacting with new situations, as there is a level of trust that derives from this, in conjunction, of course, with understanding boundaries. Remember, though, that obedience is about asking your dog to do something for you, so being in a position to expect your requests to be obeyed is a serious responsibility. In some instances, it is asking your dog to give up his interests in order to please you.

Obedience is not only about obeying a request, but about doing so quickly – that is, the first time of asking – and being able to comply even in a situation where there are distractions, or where what is being requested is in opposition to a strong motivation to do something else.

In order to do this, it's necessary to learn how to motivate puppies to comply, and then manage situations to ensure continued compliance.

This pup is giving her owner her full attention as requested. Having a reliable means of getting your pup to focus exclusively on you means you can avoid her focusing on other things which may get her into trouble.

The key cues that a pup needs to be able to comply with immediately when requested are –

- Come to me
- Walk calmly next to me
- Give me your attention
- Don't move from where I have asked you to stay
- Let go of that/spit that out

TIPS

✦ All of the tips from Life Skill 6 apply here also; for example –

- Decide on a set of cues and instructions that everyone can understand and use
- Each cue needs to be distinct
- There needs to be consistency in expectations and consequences
- Don't ask your pup to do something you know he is not yet capable of
- Manage situations where he will find it difficult to listen to you

✦ First teach your pup what action on his part pays off. Do this by using a toy or treat to encourage him to do what you want him to. For example, try running a couple of paces away from him to encourage him to move toward you (to teach the recall), or hold a treat just above his nose and move it up and back to encourage him to sit. Always reward him in a way that he likes once he is doing the action.

The following sequence of three images shows the pup focusing on the food treat in her owner's hand. As she follows the movement of the hand upward and backward with her head, her bottom automatically lowers to the ground until she is sitting. Once she follows the hand action reliably, fade out the treat enticement and just give her a treat once she is sitting. After that you can say the word 'sit' just before you use the hand gesture so that she begins to make the association between the word and the action which pays off for her.

Puppies will vary in how close your hand needs to be to their nose to elicit the required behaviour. Generally, closer to the nose is better, but there are exceptions, as this pup illustrates.

Life skills for puppies

> **REMEMBER!**
> Be careful not to use cues only when you want things to stop, for example, only ever calling him back at the end of a walk, as he will soon figure out that coming back is not good in this instance. Sometimes (when it is safe to do so) ask him to do something, for example, call him to you, and then tell him that he's free to go back to doing what he was doing (having fun!).

✦ Once he knows what action will earn him a reward, put a cue to the action so that he begins to make the association between the two (for example 'come' means get back to you for something good)

✦ When training, so that you can have complete confidence in his compliance, gradually make it more difficult for him to do as you ask. Perhaps ask him to comply with your request at a time when he is strongly motivated to do something else. At these times take precautions that will help him not to make a mistake (keep him on a lead, maybe) and make sure that the payoff for listening to you is really, really good. In this way, he will learn that paying attention to you is usually better than the other options on offer.

✦ If he makes a mistake and does not listen, don't continue to ask him, but manage the situation in whatever manner is appropriate to help him to get it right. Then build that scenario into your training so that he can get it right the next time.

REMEMBER!
Only ask him to do something when it is really important (unless you are practising, of course), and, when he complies, tell him that he has been good and make a fuss of him in a way he enjoys when he responds to you. If he does not respond, step in to manage the situation so that he does not learn that ignoring you is acceptable.

This pup has been taught to come quickly when she hears her name, and she is now being taught to leave special chews and toys when called. When you begin to ask your pup to come back in more difficult situations, make sure that you reward her with especially good stuff to convince her that it is truly worthwhile. Remember: never call your pup if you think she won't come, but instead go and fetch her so that she doesn't practise ignoring you.

LIFE SKILL 7 WORKSHEET

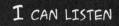 I CAN LISTEN

My puppy is learning the following behaviours –

Behaviour	Cue	Progress record
example: Give me your full attention	*'Watch me'*	*Can do it in the house where there are fewer distractions, but not in the garden yet*

· ·

· ·

· ·

· ·

· ·

· ·

· ·

· ·

· ·

· ·

· ·

· ·

· ·

· ·

· ·

· ·

I have good manners and can say "please"

Puppies need to learn socially acceptable behaviour in their interactions with people as well as with other dogs. Good manners mean a dog can be taken places and spend time with guests when people come to visit you.

Teaching good manners around people is usually relatively straightforward if you start this early. However, it is important to ensure that all people expect the same standard of behaviour as you do. Once again, consistency is the key to success and someone who gives your pup attention for jumping up makes the job of teaching him to sit politely to be greeted much more difficult.

Teaching dogs to be polite around other dogs can be a lot more complicated, because setting up the situations in which to teach this and managing other dogs in these scenarios is often challenging. Ideally, your pup should not believe that he can run up to any other dog he sees as, although this impolite behaviour may be tolerated when he is a puppy, it may be resented by other dogs as he gets older, which may lead to problems.

Good manners with people

TIPS

✦ Decide what your pup needs to do when he wants something. 'Sit' is often the easiest action to choose. Ask your pup to sit before everything that is of value to him, for example –

- Before his meals
- Before you put his lead on
- Before you open the door for him
- Before you give him attention

Teaching your puppy a means of 'saying please' to obtain things she wants is a useful way to encourage good manners. The following three images demonstrate sitting for food. First ask her to sit before feeding, and then, after a few days, simply wait with her food bowl next to you until she sits without being asked. When she does, praise her and give her the food.

This is not to prove you are boss or anything like that, but simply to teach him that polite behaviour is rewarded with things he wants. In other words, good manners are the key to good things.

Once he has practised this for a few days, wait for him to offer to sit without you having to ask. So, for example, pick up his full food bowl and just wait. As soon as he sits – and most pups will sit fairly quickly once they understand the process – tell him he's good and place the bowl on the ground. What he is now learning is to take control of being polite instead of having to be asked.

✦ Pups who learn this skill will usually start to sit whenever they want something (unless, of course, they are too excited, in which case those situations will need to be managed until he can control himself). This then becomes his polite way of asking for things. Ideally, even if you have no intention of handing over the Sunday roast as he sits hopefully in the middle of the kitchen floor, acknowledge how good he is being by giving him a little praise and attention. This will

If your puppy is struggling to keep all four paws on the ground when he greets someone, have him on a lead for greetings so that you can discourage him from practising the wrong behaviour.

reinforce the behaviour and keep it strong. Ignoring his politeness will reduce the likelihood of him repeating it.

Good manners with dogs

TIPS

✦ Make sure that your pup has a good recall, and get in the habit of calling him away from other dogs, giving him

a HUGE reward when he complies and allowing him to go back to play with his mates. Readiness to come to you when asked will mean you will have a better chance of calling him away from a situation that looks as if it may be getting out of hand.

✦ When he is young, take special toys and treats with you on walks. When he spots another dog in the distance, BEFORE he begins to run over, call him to you and reward him. Keep him close to you until you have judged whether or not a meeting with the other dog is appropriate. If it is, wait until the distance between the dogs is small enough that they can approach in a more measured way (not barreling full tilt across a field at one another). Then give him a cue such as 'say hello' and let him greet.

It's very difficult to leave your friends behind to come back to your owner when called! You can make this easier for your pup by first practising calling her when standing close to her and when the game is not too intense, and rewarding her for coming to you. Ask the other puppy's owner to call or distract their puppy away at the same time. Slowly build up to being able to call her away even from very exciting games.

LIFE SKILLS FOR PUPPIES

✦ If the other dog barrels up to your pup and this seems to make him uncomfortable, try to distract the other dog with a handful of treats tossed on the ground in front of his nose, and then immediately engage your pup in an upbeat manner and move away so that he can relax again.

✦ Generally, greeting on lead is difficult for dogs, probably as they are restricted in their ability to select an interaction distance at which they feel comfortable. If you can avoid on-lead meetings do so (see Appendix on loose lead walking and Life Skill 4 for details). If you cannot, use the 'say hello' cue as detailed in Life Skill 4 to manage the situation as best you can. No two encounters are the same, and so certain instances may call for some quick thinking.

✦ Allowing dogs to play together is generally considered valuable for many reasons, although it is vital to watch that the interaction is fun for both/all parties. True play can be identified by –

- Play bow
- Play face
- Role swapping (first one chases, then the other, first one rolls over, then the other)
- A mixture of different behaviours that do not follow a sequence, for example stalk, followed by run away, followed by chase, followed by roll over

In this picture the puppy shows a 'play face' with her mouth open and relaxed, and lips loose and not pulled back to expose the teeth. This pup is pouncing, which is another characteristic play action. It is never recommended to play with your puppy using your hands or feet as this encourages inappropriate biting or mouthing, which can be a problem later. Always play with your puppy with appropriate toys.

In a play bow (opposite), the front of the body is lowered with the bottom up in the air, sometimes all the way, as with this puppy, although it may be that only a slight front leg bend is seen. Some puppies bounce up and down or sideways at the same time. The tail is usually wagging in a wide, sweeping, relaxed manner. This pup's ears are pricked forward and her mouth is open in a relaxed manner without exposing the teeth, which also indicates play.

If it seems that not all of the dogs are having fun, interrupt the interaction and divert their attention to something else. This way, those who may be feeling uncomfortable will feel less pressurised and not develop a dislike of interaction with other dogs.

These puppies are showing another usual characteristic of play – role swapping. In the first image the Malamute is chasing; in the second it's the German Shepherd's turn. Note the relaxed faces and tails (more difficult to see in the Malamute because of her normal curled tail carriage), and the loose, gambolling gait. This relaxed movement is another indication of the friendliness of the encounter. Dogs can, of course, also growl and tense their muscles in play, but in addition to these signals, you should see some or all of the signals discussed above. Reading the interaction as a whole, as well as the ever-changing behaviour of both dogs, will help you to differentiate between play and threatening behaviour.

LIFE SKILL 8 WORKSHEET   I HAVE GOOD MANNERS AND CAN SAY "PLEASE"

My puppy is learning to ask politely for the following –

Situations where he needs to sit
example: To go out through the front door

Puppy's progress
Will sit as long as he doesn't think there's something exciting the other side of the door

. . . .

. . . .

. . . .

. . . .

. . . .

. . . .

. . . .

Politely greeting other dogs –

Situation where he meets another dog
example: He sees his dog friends in the park every day

Puppy's progress
If I keep him occupied with treats we can get close enough for him to greet politely

. . . .

. . . .

. . . .

. . . .

. . . .

. . . .

. . . .

I need help to make the right choices

Being able to choose gives a degree of control, and this is important for an individual's welfare. We should not expect our dog to be a slave to our needs if we really care about his wellbeing and our relationship with him, so this Life Skill encompasses two points.

Firstly, as an owner it is important that we do give our dog choices: where to sleep, where to sniff on a walk, who to associate with, for example. Secondly, as our dogs need to fit into the family and the society in which we live, it is important that we guide our puppies to making the correct choice in a specific situation. It is crucial to remember that, in most behavioural decisions, the pup has a choice – to do what is requested, or not; to follow the rules he knows, or not – and it's an owner's responsibility to show him that choosing the behaviour that we want is best for him, too.

TIPS

✦ Give your pup choices in everyday life. Provide a couple of comfy beds in different places, a variety of toys, if he stops to sniff on a walk allow him to take his time. You wouldn't like it if you were pulled away whilst in the middle of a conversation, which is what happens when we pull our dogs on when they have stopped to smell a 'message.'

✦ Allow your pup to choose not to approach a situation should he not want to. For example, if he backs away or

This puppy's lowered head and nose lick gesture with the eyes focused ahead indicate that she is not comfortable with the situation. If you see this sort of body language in your puppy, assess what you need to do to make her feel more comfortable. For example, if she was looking at another dog approaching her bed, call the other dog away.

I need help to make the right choices

This puppy also looks a little concerned about someone coming close to his chew. Note the ears pulled back and the muscle tension in the face with the furrows between his eyes and his tense lips. He is also shifting his body weight slightly backward: note the back leg bending and the arched back. In this case it would be advisable not to go closer to his chew, but to take a course of action to make him feel more comfortable with your presence. As an immediate step, move further away to reduce the tension while you decide how to do this.

tries to circle around or otherwise avoid a meeting, respect what your pup is telling you and respond appropriately to his needs. If the pup understands that indicating his discomfort in a given situation will mean that you intervene appropriately and remove him, he will learn that he does not need to escalate his response or become fearful or anxious.

If the situation is one that he needs to learn to accept as non-threatening, refer to Life Skill 1 to plan an introduction policy for the future so that he can successfully cope with this.

✦ Encourage behaviours that you do want. Most dogs thrive on their owner's attention, and simply acknowledging them with verbal praise and attention, or fussing them when you notice them choose an appropriate response is a valuable tool with which to reinforce that behaviour, and make it more likely that he will make the right choice next time.

For example, if you see your pup backing away from a toy that another dog is defending, tell him how clever he is to be choosing an appropriate social response rather than engaging in conflict over it. Remember, puppies are learning from every experience, so make sure they learn what you want them to. Practice really does make perfect!

✦ And once again remember not to expect your puppy to make a choice in a situation where he does not yet have the skills to do so correctly. In these situations it is important for his owner to decide and manage his choice for him. For example, if moving objects arouse him, don't take him near a busy road and expect him to choose to pay attention to you rather than try to chase the cars. If you should need to walk him near such a road, keep him on a lead and actively engage his attention, either with highly desirable treats or even by walking with him tugging on a toy to keep him engaged with you rather than lunging at the end of the lead after the cars. Later, when he has learnt self-control and loose lead walking, you can expect him to choose to attend to you rather than the traffic.

Generally, puppies prefer to settle in an out of the way corner or an enclosed bed when they need to escape from things that concern them, or simply want to rest. Provide your pup with just such a den-like space, and make sure that no-one ever disturbs her when she is there so that she can regard it as her safe haven.

Remember!

We can also encourage correct choices by intervening early in a situation, rather than waiting until your pup has already made the wrong choice. Guide your pup at the time he is THINKING about acting, not when he is already doing so.

For example, if you see him notice a dog in the distance and you're not sure that you want him to rush over to him, call him to you the moment you see him notice; don't wait until he is already moving toward the other dog. When your pup comes to you, make a huge fuss of him, possibly reward him with a treat or toy, and then, if you have decided it's safe and appropriate for him to meet the dog, give a release cue that gives him permission to approach and 'say hello.'

Guide the **INTENTION**; don't wait until you need to correct the **ACTION**.

Most puppies want to chase things that move. To prevent your puppy from lunging on the end of the lead after joggers or cyclists, teach him to play safe tug games and distract him in difficult situations by initiating a tug game while you walk.

✦ To help your pup choose to avoid conflict around the house, provide him with his own safe area – a bed, a crate, a puppy pen – which is comfortable and secure and where no-one will bother him. Teach him to associate it with good things (by providing him with special toys and treats there), and encourage him to go there when he feels happy so that he is also likely to choose it when he is worried and needs comfort.

LIFE SKILL 9 WORKSHEET

I NEED HELP TO MAKE THE RIGHT CHOICES

My puppy can make choices in the following situations –

Choices in everyday life

example: He has beds/safe places in the lounge, kitchen and bedroom, all of which are available at all times

. . . .

. . . .

. . . .

. . . .

. . . .

. . . .

. . . .

How I can guide my puppy to make the right choices –

Situation	**How I can encourage the right choice**
example: He looks worried when the neighbour's children visit and are running around	*At these times I will take a food toy to his bed and encourage him to play with it there – also ensuring that he is left in peace to do so*

. . . .

. . . .

. . . .

. . . .

. . . .

. . . .

. . . .

I have the right to be a dog and to express my opinion politely

Teaching dogs the skills they need to cope with modern human society is intended to reduce their stress as well as ensure safety for dogs and people, and strengthen the relationship they have with their owners. It is, however, vital to remember that to safeguard the welfare of the dogs who share our lives we need to ensure we meet their needs within our often busy schedules.

This final Life Skill deals with helping dogs to enjoy their right to 'be a dog.'

Puppies need time and space to be puppies, and to perform normal canine behaviours in an appropriate manner: for example, digging, chewing, sniffing, playing and running. They also need to be respected when they express an opinion such as a desire to avoid a situation or encounter. Owners can learn to read signals which indicate that their pup is uncomfortable, and allow the pup to leave the situation so that he does not feel the need to escalate his reaction.

There are numerous safe chews that you can give your puppy, including many of the strong rubber toys that are designed to hold food to encourage interest. With these, she learns to chew appropriate items, rather than your treasured possessions.

Life skills for puppies

Being a dog sometimes clashes with human values, and these differences of opinion may result in behaviour that should be recognized, acknowledged and managed, and not regarded as malicious acts to be suppressed.

TIPS

✦ Make sure that your pup's needs are met at each stage of his development. For example, puppies usually like to chew, and when their adult teeth begin to come through at between 4 and 6 months of age, are particularly in need of things to gnaw on. Be sure to provide appropriate outlets to satisfy this need and avoid probems with your pup chewing things you don't want him to.

✦ Often, puppies like to rip and shake as well as chew; suitable pieces of strong cloth and cardboard boxes (with all staples and clips removed) are inexpensive items that they can take pleasure in destroying.

If your pup shows an inclination to swallow pieces of cloth, then, of course, access to such items should be restricted to when you are able to supervise this activity.

✦ Many puppies like digging, so providing a sand pit area in the garden – just a small corner demarcated with logs or stones, and made attractive with half-buried toys and treats – can help to ensure that they don't do their digging in your flowerbeds.

Remember!

Puppies that do chew something precious or dig a hole in the lawn are not doing so to be spiteful or to 'get back' at you. They are simply performing a behaviour that makes them feel good and they have not yet learnt that it's not appropriate to do so in these places.

✦ Dogs need interaction and mental stimulation as well as physical exercise, so it's very important ensure that they can

continued page 74

This sequence of images shows a puppy that has been given a cardboard box containing a few treats to play with. The idea is to direct her interest in ripping, tearing and shaking to something appropriate. Always make sure that you remove any metal staples or clips, and any plastic tape before giving a box to a puppy.

This puppy in the next three images has been given an interactive food ball to play with. It is quite acceptable – and in fact recommended – to feed your pup some or all of his meals from food dispensing toys, as this directs his mental and physical energy in appropriate directions. Always make sure that the toy is tough enough to withstand chewing, and that you teach your pup how it works to avoid excessive frustration!

Although this is not a toy you would leave with your unsupervised pup, hiding treats under a plastic lid keeps this pup busy in interactive play. You can also build a self-control element into this game by asking your pup to sit while you reset the lid each time he has managed to tip it over.

engage in games, get attention from people, and are taken for safe walks, all on a daily basis.

✦ Respect what your pup is telling you and respond appropriately to his needs. If your pup learns that indicating his discomfort in a given situation will result in you intervening and removing him from it, this means that he does not need to become more fearful or anxious, or learn an inappropriate way of dealing with the situation, such as escalating to a threat.

Occasionally, when pups feel uneasy about something, they may bark or even run away. However, most pups will hang back, try to move aside, hide, or

display even more subtle signs which indicate discomfort (remember, all behaviour is context-specific, so take care with interpretations), and may include –

- Glancing away or squinting
- Turning his head aside or lowering his head
- Licking his lips
- Yawning
- Tucking his ears back
- Tucking his tail in
- Sniffing the ground

If, when you see any of these signs, you give your pup a chance to move away from the situation until he is relaxed,

We can tell that this pup is uncomfortable by her lowered head and staring focus, the body leaning back over the hind legs and the tense muscles, clearly seen in the tail which is starting to tuck.

A nose lick can mean different things, but with this puppy – combined with tense lips, a dropped head and eyes focused forward – it should be interpreted as indicative of discomfort. Many puppies find a hand reaching over their head or neck quite threatening.

The tense facial muscles seen in the lips pulled forward, the ears flattened against the head, the arched back with the pup apparently pulling into herself, and the focused staring eyes all tell you that this puppy is very uncomfortable. At this point, the action to take is to move away to give the pup space, and allow her then to approach in her own time.

or until he has developed better coping skills, you will reduce the need for him to growl, snap or even bite.

NEVER reprimand or punish your puppy for being uneasy, avoiding a situation or showing aggression, as this will make matters worse, and he does not deserve the punishment. Simply remove him from the situation until he is calm, and try to work out why he is unhappy. Seek professional help if you are in any doubt.

Remember!

Try always to see the world from your pup's point of view (and level), and remember to always encourage any behaviour that is appropriate. Puppies learn from every experience, so make sure they learn what you want them to.

I have the right to be a dog and to express my opinion politely

You and your puppy can both have a great deal of fun playing games with appropriate toys.

LIFE SKILL 10 WORKSHEET

I HAVE THE RIGHT TO BE A DOG ...

My puppy's needs have been met in the following ways –

Things my pup has available to meet his needs and ensure his wellbeing
examples: Areas in the house which provide a safe haven
A variety of toys which I rotate to retain his interest

. . . .

. . . .

. . . .

. . . .

. . . .

. . . .

. . . .

Times when my pup expresses his opinion

Situation
example: Met a man wearing a high visibility jacket and puppy backed away

How I managed it
I moved a few feet away until he had relaxed again, and let him watch for a while. He then walked on quite happily

. . . .

. . . .

. . . .

. . . .

. . . .

. . . .

I hope my person remembers that ...

- Dogs are not machines (they make mistakes and like to explore rule boundaries)
- Dogs have feelings
- Dogs need to be taught patiently and calmly
- Dogs don't understand English so people need to understand dog

- Dogs are not malicious; they simply do what works for them
- Dogs are not motivated by dominance but like to work with friends
- Dogs are very observant and are learning all the time
- Having a dog takes time

This person has understood the reason for the slightly worried look on the pup's face as they bend over her on her bed, and is helping her feel more comfortable by approaching from the side, rather than reaching over her head, and feeding her a treat (overleaf).

- Dogs need a balance of activity and calm
- Obedience is not the same as being well behaved; dogs need to learn both
     But most importantly, I hope you will remember

that, although building a relationship with your dog may take effort, the rewards on offer make every single moment worth it!

I hope my person remembers that ...

A useful first step in teaching your puppy to settle down on her bed when asked is to teach her to lie down on cue, as demonstrated by the following image sequence (and overleaf). To entice your puppy into a down position, start by using a treat held just above her nose to encourage your pup into a sitting position, and then slowly drop your hand down in front of her, close to her chest, to encourage her to bend her front legs to the ground whilst keeping her bottom on the floor. Teaching this requires patience as some pups need lots of intermediate treats (as the elbows bend more and more) to help them understand what's required.

Loose lead walking

Being able to walk with your dog on a lead without him pulling you along makes your life together much more enjoyable for you both. However, loose lead walking is a skill which can take a while to master, and to do so it's very important that you apply your chosen training technique consistently over time. Without consistency, your pup will become confused and most likely decide that paying no attention to you and lots to the environment is the best option – which then, of course, usually results in pulling.

There are many different ways to teach dogs to walk nicely on a lead, and as long as the technique you choose keeps in mind your dog's welfare, it's up to you to determine the method that best suits you both.

The following is a suggestion for a training technique which we find works well. It is an amalgamation of a number of different ideas learnt from numerous sources over the years.

The aim of this training technique is to enable your pup to walk with you without pulling, whilst still enjoying the walk and the environment as he has learnt to divide his attention between you and his surroundings. Of course, you should both enjoy the walk as we regard loose lead walking as a partnership between person and dog: a contract in which your dog's undertaking is not to pull and not to trip you, and yours is to allow your dog to enjoy the walk by doing the things he likes – sniffing bushes, investigating holes, greeting people, etc. This technique is NOT intended to teach heelwork for competition.

✦ Begin with an appropriately fitting flat collar, harness or head halter attached to a lead which is of sufficient length so that your dog can walk comfortably alongside you with slack in the lead between your hand and him

✦ Decide on which side you would like your dog to walk

✦ Arm yourself with tasty, easily swallowed treats that are cut up very small (cheese, for example, or chicken or frankfurter cut into cubes of about quarter of an inch)

✦ Find a quiet, distraction-free, safe environment in which to work

✦ Attach the lead to your pup's collar or harness and stand still

✦ Say nothing, and as soon as your pup pays you attention, tell him he's good and feed him a treat

✦ Now use a treat in your fingers to bring your pup into position at your side

✦ Make sure the lead is slack and that there is no pressure on the pup's collar/harness: the lead is simply a safety line, not a means of directing his movement

✦ Feed your pup a couple more treats for standing next to you (if he sits or lies down that's ok)

✦ Take a step forward and, as your pup moves with you, feed him another treat. Don't wait for him to get ahead of you, try to feed him for managing to stay alongside you
  • If he doesn't want to move forward with you, use another treat to entice him into position next to you again

Before starting to walk, reward your puppy for simply standing next to you and paying attention to you.

Initially reward your puppy frequently (every step or two) for walking next to you and paying attention to you.

✦ If he moves along keeping pace with you, feed him a couple more treats as you slowly take a few steps forward

✦ After practicing this for a few days, ask him to walk a little further before receiving a treat, so that it isn't quite as easy for him

✦ If, at any time, he gets ahead of you or becomes distracted and pulls sideways or backward, stand still immediately, don't say anything, and wait for his attention to return to you. Once you have this, use a treat in your fingers or hand gesture to return him to your side, and have him walk a couple of steps next to you before receiving a treat

● Remember, he doesn't have to be glued to your leg, but simply moving *with* you and not pulling

As soon as your puppy pulls ahead of you, stop and stand still.

Don't begin moving again, even if your puppy pulls hard on the lead to try to get to something that interests her.

- Take care not to feed him a treat immediately he comes back to you as this can very quickly teach him that the fastest way to get a treat is to pull away and then return

✦ Repeat this initial training in different places, with gradually increasing distractions.
  Practise this until he can walk alongside you for up to about 20 paces without pulling before giving a treat,

and if he does pull, can return to position to be able to move forward

✦ At this point, for most dogs, moving forward begins to become a more important reward than the food, so you can try to fade out the food rewards, though still use them in very distracting places to help him to get it right

✦ When you reach this stage of training, you may find that

85

Once your puppy is back at your side and paying you attention, resume moving forward.

your pup develops the very annoying habit of yo-yo-ing on the lead; pulling and then coming back so that your walk becomes a stop/start affair. In this case, the next part of the training becomes very important

✦ Next time your pup pulls and then moves back into position, DON'T continue forward. You'll probably find that your pup anticipates that you will move forward and bounces forward to pull again. Stand still

✦ At this point what you want your pup to understand is that he has to be with you *mentally* before he can move forward. In other words, he has to be paying you real attention, and be in tune with you, to be able to move forward, not focusing totally on the environment and just flicking you a look now and again

✦ Judging this mental state can be difficult, but look for signs that your pup has moved his attention from the environment and firmly back to you. Some dogs demonstrate this by sitting next to you, some show a more relaxed posture instead of being intently focused on the environment, some make sustained eye contact with you

✦ When you see this change in behaviour, tell him he is very good and move forward again

✦ It may be beneficial to use food rewards again for a while here so that the change in mental attitude receives two payoffs – food and movement – but DON'T give in to the temptation to use a treat to move him into position. At this point we want your pup to take responsibility for walking without pulling, which means that it will no longer be necessary for you to manage him as he will have learnt to manage himself

(and pages 88 & 89) In the early stages of training use a treat to tempt your pup to move back to your side. Later, just use a hand signal and eventually expect your pup to be able to move back on her own.

✦ With time he will develop the skill of paying you just enough attention to match his pace to yours and change direction with you whilst still enjoying his surroundings. At this point he won't be actively looking at you at all (or very rarely), but will simply be keeping you in his peripheral vision

✦ This aspect of training will take time, and may need to be recapped at times when your pup's attention may falter: for example, if he is in an exciting place, or has been ill and not had a walk for a few days. And, of course, as with all adolescents, when he goes through his teenage months (around the time of puberty) he may well need a gentle reminder of the rules.

Now you should be able to experience walks with your pup without him pulling. Enjoy!

Important note

Should you at any time need to move your pup quickly from a situation, take the lead very short, right next to his collar/harness, get his attention by saying his name, and hold it by talking to him intermittently. In this way you can get him to move quickly and calmly out of a tricky situation. If you have a treat you can also entice him to walk close to you rather than taking a short lead, and use a cue word such as 'close' to indicate to him that he needs to move with you quickly.

Using a treat is a useful way to move your pup into the position you want him to be in, although you should not rely on this method for too long as your pup may then learn to pay attention only when he can see food. Move fairly quickly from treats to a hand gesture to direct action (and later a word, if you prefer) and use the treats only AFTER he has performed the action, as a reward.

Rogues' Gallery: the Cast

Nelson:
Portugese
Podengo

Griff:
Australian Shepherd x
Border Collie

Jack: Whippet

Kya: German Shepherd Dog

Toffee: Nova
Scotia Duck
Tolling Retriever x
Brittany Spaniel

Alfie: Cavalier King
Charles Spaniel

Kira: Alaskan
Malamute

Phoebe: Boxer

Poppy: Border Terrier

Chi-Chi: Pomerarian x
Chihuahua

91

Lots more Hubble and Hattie books for you to enjoy!

128 pages
100 colour ills
ISBN: 9781845843571
£12.99*

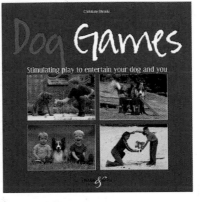

128 pages
245 colour ills
ISBN: 9781845843328
£15.99*

128 pages
100 colour ills
ISBN: 9781845843229
£12.99*

128 pages
101 mainly colour ills
ISBN: 9781845844103
£12.99*

128 pages
137 colour ills
ISBN: 9781845843410
£12.99*

96 pages
50 colour ills
ISBN: 9781845843809
£9.99*

Dogs on wheels — Travelling with your canine companion

RAC — the driving people

n Mort

80 pages
90 colour Ills
9781845843793
£9.99*

CLEVER DOG!

LIFE LESSONS FROM THE WORLD'S MOST SUCCESSFUL ANIMAL

- MASTER SALESMAN
- MASTER SURVIVOR
- MASTER TACTICIAN

- MASTER NEGOTIATOR
- MASTER LISTENER

- MASTER OPPORTUNIST
- MASTER OF INTEGRITY

RYAN O'MEARA

Hubble & Hattie

96 pages
11 ills
9781845843458
£9.99*

YOU AND YOUR Border Terrier

David Alderton

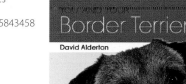

THE Essential GUIDE

96 pages
100 colour Ills
9781845843193
£9.99*

dog SPEAK

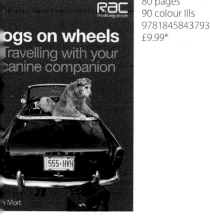

ognising and derstanding aviour

Hubble & Hattie

80 pages
139 colour ills
9781845843847
£9.99*

DOG RELAX — relaxed dogs, relaxed owners

Sabina Pilguj

Hubble & Hattie

144 pages
144 colour ills
9781845843335
£7.99*

YOU AND YOUR Cockapoo

David Alderton

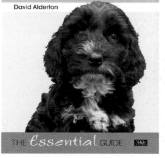

THE Essential GUIDE

96 pages
100 colour ills
9781845843205
£9.99*

Dieting with my DOG

ONE BUSY LIFE, TWO FULL FIGURES ... AND UNCONDITIONAL LOVE

y Frezon

Hubble & Hattie

112 pages
30 colour ills
9781845844066
£9.99*

SMELLORAMA! — Nose games for dogs

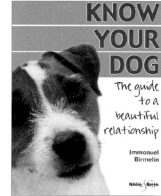

80 pages
38 col & 35 b&w ills
9781845842932
£9.99*

KNOW YOUR DOG

The guide to a beautiful relationship

Immanuel Birmelin

Hubble & Hattie

96 pages
76 colour ills
9781845840723
£4.99*

LOTS MORE HUBBLE AND HATTIE BOOKS FOR YOU TO ENJOY!

my DOG **IS BLIND**
– but lives life to the full!

The guide to every aspect of a happy life with a blind or sight-impaired dog

Hubble & Hattie

ISBN: 9781845842918

my DOG has **ARTHRITIS**
– but lives life to the full!

A practical guide for owners

Hubble & Hattie

ISBN: 9781845844189

All 80 pages and between 50 and 60 colour ills. £9.99* each

ISBN: 9781845843823

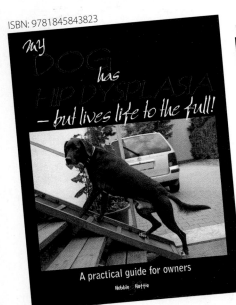

my DOG has **HIP DYSPLASIA**
– but lives life to the full!

A practical guide for owners

Hubble & Hattie

ISBN: 9781845843816

my DOG **IS DEAF**
– but lives life to the full!

A practical guide for owners

Hubble & Hattie

ISBN: 9781845843830

my DOG has a **CRUCIATE LIGAMENT INJURY**
– but lives life to the full!

A practical guide for owners

Hubble & Hattie

The truth wolves dogs

DISPELLING THE MYTHS OF DOG TRAINING

Hubble&Hattie

TONI SHELBOURNE

IS MY DOG A WOLF?

112 pages
126 colour ills
ISBN: 9781845844271
£12.99*

208 pages 200 colour ills
ISBN: 9781845844295
£6.99*

EMERGENCY FIRST AID FOR DOGS

At home and away

Hubble&Hattie

64 pages 43 colour ills
ISBN: 9781845843861 £4.99*

RAC the driving people

Walking the dog
French motorway walks for drivers and dogs

Lezli Rees

RAC the driving people

Walking the dog
Motorway walks for drivers and dogs

Lezli Rees

208 pages 200 colour ills
ISBN: 9781845841027
£4.99*

For more info on Hubble and Hattie books please visit www.hubbleandhattie.com;
email info@hubbleandhattie.com; tel 44 (0) 1305 260068. *prices subject to change

Index